Every Parent's Dilemma

Every Parent's Dilemma

Why Do We Ignore Schools That Nurture Children?

by

DON BERG

Founder of Schools of Conscience

Order this book online at www.trafford.com
or email orders@trafford.com

Most Trafford titles are also available at major online book retailers.

Print information available on the last page.

ISBN: 978-1-4907-4345-5 (sc)
ISBN: 978-1-4907-4344-8 (e)

Library of Congress Control Number: 2014917103

Trafford rev. 01/06/2015

 www.trafford.com

North America & international
toll-free: 1 888 232 4444 (USA & Canada)
fax: 812 355 4082

Contents

Every Parent's Dilemma:
Why Do We Ignore Schools That Nurture Children?

What is wrong with the school is what is wrong with the family is what is wrong with society. We are a society that has failed to gear itself to enable people to meet their basic needs.

James P. Comer, *What I Learned In School* p.49 (Jossey-Bass, 2009)

K-12 schools are failing to nurture our children. But to hear the mainstream media tell it, you would think that the key problems of our K-12 system are either funding issues, diversity issues, or technical issues of pedagogy and accountability for achieving specified academic results. They do not even realize that nurturing is required, yet is absent. When critics notice how difficult circumstances (socioeconomic or otherwise) impair the capacity of parents to nurture their children, the critics mysteriously neglect to consider that a nurturing response by schools might be warranted.

Today the vast majority of parents default to entrusting schools with the care of their children for most of the waking hours of childhood, yet they too fail to consider a nurturing response to the evident difficulties schools have in fulfilling their duties to children. There are reasons for the absence of these basic considerations of nurturing, by both critics and parents, but it is time to put this ignorance behind us. Our children are not being supported, while they are in school, to meet their primary human needs or "basic needs," as Yale University's Dr. Comer calls them in the quote above. Unless we take corrective action, the lack of nurturing will surely become a monumental disaster for our society.

Fortunately, there is a growing vanguard of both individuals and organizations who have been pioneering nurturing responses in K-12, myself included. We are a small and fractious minority. Education researchers, an elite club I joined in 2011, have only recently taken our programs seriously enough to study them and early findings suggest a scientific vindication of our faith in nurturing through facilitation of self-directed learning. Our proclamations about the benefits of nurturing have been falling on deaf ears for too long. It is time for us to come together to deliver the nurturing message in a new way that can enable all of society to benefit from what we have accomplished.

I have been involved with K-12 self-directed learning communities in the forms of democratic schools, home schooling, and non-school learning communities for over 20 years. These education alternatives have been around for over 100 years, and today all of them put together serve less than 5% of the K-12 student population in the United States (see Appendix 1: Estimating Our Influence). Given how few students in the United States attend schools that support it, the influence of self-directed learning in K-12 is limited and substantive support is in short supply. K-12 programs that support self-directed learning are rare. Self-directed learning programs that receive public funding are a rarity amongst the rare; they are vanishingly scarce. When they dare to access public funds, they are under constant threat of being arbitrarily required to make important learning decisions for children, being made to take control of children's time and attention in ways that are detrimental to the children, or summarily closed by bureaucrats who don't understand them. Self-directed learning programs usually choose to rely on scarce private funding as a form of self-defense, thereby also reducing their accessibility.

These hazards and limitations to self-directed learning programs stem from the default, naïve concept of education that has guided almost all schooling from its inception thousands of years ago. Since the 1980's, the hazards and limitations to self-directed learning programs have been made worse by a political consensus on the necessity of imposing testing and standardization. That consensus is simply extending the logic of the default, naïve concept of education to a post-industrial mass-market scale. Dr. Yong Zhao, Professor of Education at the University of Oregon, in his 2012 book *World Class Learners* shows how effectively imposing national standards and high stakes testing, as China and other Asian countries have been doing for decades, destroys creativity and entrepreneurship along with all of the key characteristics that current business leaders say they want schools to instill in their future employees. Most people are not like you and me; they have no experience with a school that facilitates self-directed learning or know that families who successfully home school are not merely re-creating the conditions of school at home. Most people have probably never even considered self-directed learning for K-12 students, nor its challenges.

My experience with successful alternatives came out of my own discovery of a passion to work with school-age children. I knew from my experience as a public school student in highly-regarded schools, magnet programs and districts that the classroom was not a good learning environment for me. It did not seem plausible that the classroom would be any better on the other side of the teacher's desk. Later, I became a "teacherpreneur" home schooling other people's kids. In the absence of a sustainable business model, I decided to return to school in 2010 to complete the psychology degree that I had started back in the 1980's in the midst of discovering my passion. My thesis research was a study of the patterns of motivation in the Village Home Education Resource Center (which operates like a community college for K-12) and the Village Free School (a democratic day school). That research was published in 2013 in the international peer-reviewed journal *Other Education*.[1]

Numerous studies of the patterns of motivation, engagement, and mental health of students in traditional schools have shown decreases in well-being.[2] My thesis is one of very few published studies demonstrating that there *are* schools that actually support the psychological well-being of K-12 students. The first peer-reviewed published evidence was a study of EdVisions Charter Schools in 2009.[3] On the other hand, the Yale School Development Program (SDP) has been demonstrating for over 40 years[4] that supporting the well-being of children within the school environment is a vital part of successful reform efforts, especially for schools that serve a high proportion of students from marginalized populations. The SDP has focused on three things: pervasively building positive relationships throughout school communities (a primary human need, which I will explain later), ensuring that the developmental needs of children inform school decision-making, and viewing schools as complex systems rather than just a relatively simple accumulation of individual interactions. (SDP, however, does not appear to have incorporated the systematic collection of data on patterns of motivation, engagement, nor the mental health of students.) Many other schools and programs, like the Yale SDP, probably incorporate some of the key elements of support that I will explain later. In fact, I am confident that there are other schools supporting psychological well-being, but I can't be sure because there are no published data of the right kind to support my confidence.

Support for self-directed learning is a major factor that distinguishes psychologically supportive schools from those that are not. The distinction I make between self-directed and non-self-directed learning is determined by how much effective power the students have in directing their own activities. In the case of homeschooling, children have a lot of effective power because they have direct access to the primary decision makers for their education and can exert influence on them independent of how family members think or talk about the family's homeschooling practices. The self-directed learning programs I have experienced and studied have a diversity of systems for ensuring that their students can make many decisions at a variety of time-scales in order to learn how to be successful participants both within those particular communities and in the world at large. Each school or program is a response to the challenge of ensuring that the community's structuring of student choices encourages children to start wherever they are presently at and over time develop ever longer time-scales of commitment to accomplishing self-selected goals that are interesting and valuable.

Very young, very impulsive, and very insecurely attached students usually need shorter time-scales of choice than others. It is obvious to anyone with experience relating to children of various ages that a two-year-old operates at a different time scale than a teenager. This means that "effective power" depends on the developmental, dispositional, and relational contexts in which the student is embedded. A school or program has to have structures that take those contextual factors into account (implicitly, at least) in order to produce a functional outcome for both individual student development and the safety and sanity of their fellow community members.

Non-self-directed learning, on the other hand, limits the effective power of students participating in the school community by pre-determining many goals and imposing arbitrary limits on a) the number of decisions that students are allowed to make, b) the available timescales in which student decisions can occur, and c) the scope of planning that will be supported (often with little or no reference or access to the world at large). The non-self-directed learning end of this continuum is the default, the status quo, in traditional schools today, independent of their funding sources, organizational structure, or legal status.

In 20 years from 1991 to 2011, charter schools grew to serve over two million students in the United States[5] (approximately 4%). This was true despite charter schools being dominated by the status quo of non-self-directed learning.[6] The charter school movement was intended to be an engine of educational innovation, yet the kind of innovation that actually makes a psychological difference for students may be represented only marginally better in the population of public charter schools than in the population of regular public schools. The growth of our self-directed learning programs seems stunted compared with what the charter movement has proved is possible, and it will continue to be stunted if nothing changes.

Our marginalization and threats to our integrity arise from the fact that self-directed learning is still a radical concept in K-12 education. To be more accurate, it is a radical concept in terms of how schools are organized and administered as a large-scale system. I have talked with teachers extensively about motivation both in my scientific research and informally over many years before that. I have gotten the impression that they all understood that self-directed learners enable teachers to achieve their maximum effectiveness and efficiency. I suspect that the positive value of self-directed learning is universally recognized by teachers. However, there is an abundance of policies, and more importantly, an even greater abundance of implicit assumptions and practices in the school system, that actively undermine self-directed learning. To put it another way, there is a pervasive hidden curriculum that undermines self-directed learning and prevents the development of the systemic supports that are necessary for the replication and proliferation of K-12 self-directed learning programs.

Hidden Curriculum

The hidden curriculum is a concept that critics of schools have used to discuss factors that influence behavior in the classroom that are not immediately evident in the activities that occur there. The basic concept was referred to (without the term) at least as early as 1916 in John Dewey's seminal book *Democracy and Education*. The most widespread use of the term seems to be in discussions of how racism and other oppressions are perpetuated in schools. Given that it is "hidden," it will strike some that the solution to a problematic hidden curriculum is to "expose" it, which should logically eliminate it as a "hidden" factor. It is undoubtedly true that the hidden curriculum is problematic because it perpetuates oppression; however, it is also true that the nature of the hidden curriculum is such that "exposure" is not a solution. A central finding of cognitive psychology is that there are aspects of human functioning that are simply outside of our awareness and cannot be meaningfully brought into our awareness. By that I mean that individually we do not have the capability of consciously manipulating mental processes that are non-conscious even when we are made aware of how our behavioral responses are altered by certain conditions in our environment. Let me give you an example:

Here is a picture of my face. Now I am going to give you two sets of instructions. First, in any way you can, stop looking at my face. Easy, huh? All you had to do was look away or close your eyes. Notice that you were able to make an autonomous decision independent of whether or not you obeyed my command.

Now I want you to look at the picture of my face again. But this time, while continuing to see my mouth, my cheeks, and my eyes, use only your force of mental willpower to stop seeing my nose. No matter how hard you try you will not succeed. This is an impossible request to comply with due to the hidden curriculum of irreducible facial recognition processes in the brain. All human brains are hard wired to see faces as whole experiences. There is no way that a human being can volitionally control what aspects of the visual experience of a face to see or not. Thus my instruction, as presented, is impossible to comply with. It is also true that your awareness of the fact that human brains have irreducible facial recognition processes does nothing to allow you to change your experience of faces. Exposing this hidden curriculum does nothing to change it.

Similar to the brain processes that make faces irreducible experiences, there are other brain processes that also shape our experiences of certain kinds of social situations. For instance, when we perceive an instructor using controlling language, rigid deadlines, coercive discipline, and rewards to enforce boundaries, then our brain automatically reduces the quality of our attention; if it is a consistent pattern, then we will develop more anxiety, depression, or other symptoms of psychological distress. When we perceive an instructor behaving in these ways, then whatever lesson they are teaching (and everything else they are doing) becomes tainted by the hidden curriculum imposed by our brain's automatic reactions to those social cues.

This is critically important to understand because the mainstream K-12 school system is guilty of presenting most children with behavioral demands that are impossible for them to comply with due to the primacy of their needs for autonomy, competence, and relatedness. When state and federal legislatures force children into situations in which these needs are routinely thwarted, then they are putting those children in the way of psychological harm. The children are fully justified in taking action to avoid harm. Unfortunately, avoidance in this context takes the forms of dropping out, underachievement, or fauxchievement (which I will explain later). This is the one critical point of my work that is beyond doubt based on the amazing consistency of the empirical evidence: K-12 schools must stop thwarting the primary needs of the children (and all the other human beings in the system) and start supporting them to satisfy those needs instead.

Rather than simply rail against the injustice of "the System" and how our self-directed learning communities might be victims of it, I have to point out that our self-directed learning communities also share many of the implicit assumptions that undermine us. As long as we continue to unconsciously use the default, naïve conception of education or mere logical negations of assumptions that follow from it, we undermine our own ability to effectively neutralize the threats against us and address the barriers to our growth. Ironically, we celebrate critics who decry how the hidden curriculum of mainstream schools has maintained oppressions in society. Yet we have not turned the concept of the "hidden curriculum" into a lens for self-reflection on the lack of our own effectiveness as an influence on those systems. We, who champion self-directed learning, all know that we need to marshal political, economic, and social support for our cause, but there are hidden factors that we have to overcome before we can be substantially more effective at building our capacity to influence the education system. This book concludes with a suggestion for beginning to shift the pervasive hidden curriculum of the school system towards supporting self-directed learning. The strategy is to lobby policy makers based on promoting our programs as the embodiment of a new foundation for understanding education. There will always be a pervasive hidden curriculum within the system; the question is, how can we realign it to stop thwarting the primary human needs of the people who make up the system and get it to start supporting them to satisfy their needs instead?

How can we use the concept of the hidden curriculum to help us improve our ability to influence the system? If K-12 self-directed learning communities are such good educational environments, then why has growth been so difficult? Why aren't the majority of charter schools self-directed learning communities? Why aren't they like the EdVisions charter network with over 40 schools in 10 states? Why can't Village Home go back to being an alternative program within their local school districts? Why have both Village Home and the Village Free School had to struggle so hard (and mostly failed) to get the kind of financial backing that other kinds of schools routinely get? I will not presume to speak about the specific reasons for difficulties in particular programs, but I will address the broad issue of why all self-directed learning programs (not just the ones I've named) run into the same fundamental barrier even though the manifestations of the hidden curriculum for each program may look different.

A Paradigm Is The Fundamental Barrier

Consider the possibility that education is in the same position today as medicine was in the mid-1800's. In 1848, London authorities passed the "Nuisances Removal and Disease Prevention Act".[7] This was a large public investment effectively endorsing the miasma theory of

11

disease. The problem was that London stank; the city had raw sewage running in its streets. The act authorized a large-scale sewer project to wash that annoying sewage directly into the Thames River. It was perfectly logical. The policy makers reasoned that since bad smells, called miasma, were such a nuisance *and* caused disease, then getting all that filth off the streets was vitally important. The subsequent system was successful at alleviating some of the stench, but more importantly, it also quickly and substantially increased the volume of human effluent that was deposited in the drinking water of over two-thirds of the residents of the city. Epidemics of cholera subsequently killed tens of thousands of people and were far worse than they might have been *because* of that large public investment endorsing the miasma theory of disease.

Miasma theory was not merely a single idea. It was the central defining feature of a whole suite of concepts, a paradigm that provided explanations for both health and disease. The miasma idea logically lead to several competing varieties of humoral theories in Europe and other theories about the flow of bodily energies in Asia. Those various types of theories gave us the most preferred medical treatments from the pre-germ theory era: blood-letting, purging (inducing vomiting, sweating, and evacuation of the bowels), and cupping (in which a specially-shaped glass was heated and applied to the skin such that when the glass cooled a vacuum was created to "extract" harmful substances). The miasmatic theories of healing and the treatments that followed from them appeared to be effective because numerous people subjected to the treatments got better. But, miasma theory was a paradigm that misinformed the everyday thinking of both experts and lay people alike about the actual causes of health and disease.

There are important figures in the long history of the development of germ theory that suffered greatly because of the incompatibility between the dominant miasma paradigm and its eventual successor. Ignaz Semmelweiss is a particularly dramatic example; in the 1840's, by the careful collection and analysis of empirical data, he developed a successful method for reducing the deaths of his patients, mothers who had just given birth. Despite his thoroughly scientific method and the dramatic practical evidence that he was in fact saving the lives of his patients, he was both professionally and personally ridiculed and his methods rejected until long after his death in 1865. The deaths of literally thousands of new mothers over the decades between Semmelweiss' pioneering work with antiseptic procedures and the final acceptance of them as a standard medical practice means all those women (not to mention all the other preventable deaths) that occurred during that period were victims of the power of a dominant paradigm.

After the more accurate germ theory became the dominant model of disease in the late 1800's, public health improved (London stopped having epidemics of cholera, for instance), and effective medical interventions such as antibiotic drugs were widely implemented in the 1900's. The shift in the foundational cultural understanding of health and disease took decades to unfold. After public policy became aligned with the paradigm of germ theory, not only were effective public health measures implemented, but previously inconceivable treatments that would have been considered medical miracles in 1848 have now become everyday occurrences.[8]

The delivery theory of education is currently the dominant idea, the paradigm-defining idea, that determines how our school system operates.[9] It is a default, naïve conception. The delivery theory is a model of education that claims that the movement of information into the student's head is the central, defining feature of learning. Policy makers reason quite logically that accounting for the delivery is what matters, so making a school's access to relevant resources contingent on the measurement of what content is in each student's head is a perfectly logical school management strategy. Standardization also makes perfect sense according to this model, since you would want to make the instructional bookkeeping process as simple as possible; having standard units to measure is as simple as it gets. The intuitive logic of this concept is compelling and has resulted in the apparent political consensus that requiring standardized tests and imposing curriculum standards are necessary mechanisms for school improvement. Hundreds of billions of dollars in public investment[10] in the United States have endorsed this theory of education in the forms of federal legislation that mandate high stakes testing and make federal funding contingent on instructional bookkeeping. Unfortunately, like the miasma theory of disease, the delivery theory is wrong. And the paradigm that is informed by that theory is the key element of the hidden curriculum of the education system that limits the influence of our K-12 self-directed learning communities.

The nature of the error in both cases is not intuitively evident. Miasma is an intuitively powerful idea because it is true that the incidence of disease is strongly correlated with the incidence of unpleasant odors. Rotting dead things and effluent, from human populations and our animals, are harbingers of bad outcomes which, naturally, we normally seek to avoid. But as multiple millions of us, and the variety of animals that accompanied us, gathered into cities without adequate public health infrastructure, those harbingers became unavoidable. Some early cities with large populations, in spite of incorrect intuitive notions about disease and health, accidentally avoided creating the worst conditions for the spread of epidemic diseases. But the actual and immediate causal factor in disease is germs, not the smells that happen to coincidentally occur under similar conditions (nor demons, ghosts, evil spirits, curses, etc.). Smells correlate with disease, but they do not cause it. Disease-causing germs are *hidden* in the conditions that also produce bad smells. Independent of the relative success of the various intuitive ideas about disease and health that people arrived at before germ theory, it was only after the development of germ theory that we humans became accurate predictors of the consequences of our investments in the prevention of disease. That ability to accurately predict epidemiological outcomes enabled cities to routinely support multiple millions of people and animals. It has been the global adoption of public health measures consistent with the germ theory paradigm that has effectively prevented the well-known epidemic diseases, like cholera, from periodically decimating large cities since the late 1800's. It was only after we realized how specific *hidden* factors in the situations of sewage and decomposition determine both smells and disease that we became effective rather than lucky in designing public health infrastructure.

Information delivery correlates with education, but does not cause it. Education-causing cognition is *hidden* in the conditions that also produce information delivery. The cartography theory, explained below, enables us to realize how *hidden* factors in the situation of learning determine both information delivery and education. We can become far more effective at preventing ignorance if we are equipped with this distinction between the causal and the correlational factors in education.

The nature of the error in delivery theory is not intuitively evident. The delivery theory of education is powerful because easy access to informational content is highly correlated with what we mean when we consider a person to be educated. Schooling operating within the delivery paradigm appears somewhat effective since numerous people who have been subjected to it end up being educated. An educated person does, in fact, have to have access to a substantial amount of informational content in order to think and act productively. But the actual and immediate causal factor in education is the cognitive arrangement of the relationships between content, goals, and available resources. To put it more simply, what matters in education is how a person makes mental maps of their relationship to their goals, resources, and informational content. This is what I call the cartography theory of education.[11]

Imagine that you have a boat on the Willamette River in Portland, Oregon, and you want me to help you to get to Seattle, Washington. If my standardized response to requests for navigational help is to give out a map of the Oregon Trail from 1848, then I would not be helpful to you. That's what we have now in K-12 education. The system is designed to provide a standardized response to every student, but that standardized response does not account for a) the learners' goals, b) the resources that the learners have access to in order to accomplish their goals, nor, c) where each learner is positioned in relation to their goals and available resources. As a result, the standardized solutions can only serve those who coincidently happen to be in the place where the system designers thought they should be or are close enough that adaptations to their situation might work if they can figure out how to make the appropriate adaptations.

Self-directed learning within a well-structured community, on the other hand, is like having a fully functional iPad with Google Maps in which you can get routes for any transportation mode or combination of modes to which you happen to have access. By giving you the ability to plug in your own goals and available resources, the system provides a customized solution. If I gave you that kind of device, you would be able to navigate not just to Seattle, but to anywhere else you wanted to go in the future as well. What our self-directed learning communities have pioneered are a variety of ways that a school can be sensitive to the context of the learner's goals and the resources they happen to have available in order to provide customized instruction.

Inadequate concepts are a driving force behind the hidden curriculum of all schooling in the world today. Notice that I did not qualify that statement about the driving force. My claim is that even self-directed learning communities are currently being misguided by the delivery theory of education and other inadequate concepts that are derived from it. Contradictions naturally arise from thinking about our practices using an idea (or its logical negation) that does not adequately describe our effectiveness as providers of education. The left side of the table below entitled "Dominant Concepts and Potential Replacements in K-12 Dialogue" offers a variety of ideas that are sometimes used as explanatory contrasts or images in educational discourse and that I suspect cause communication problems. We get trapped in an unproductive conversation every time we take the bait by accepting these false contrasts or distorted images. This inability to communicate effectively is why self-directed learning communities of all kinds have been relatively ineffective at capturing market share and are considered radical, in spite of how obvious it is to all teachers that self-directed learners are the best students.

Dominant Concepts and Potential Replacements in K-12 Dialogue	
Unproductive Conversations and Images	**Potential Alternatives**
Academic Curriculum vs. No Curriculum	Attitude Curriculum
Back-to-Basics vs. Touchy Feely	Competence Supportive
Behaviorism vs. Humanism	Embodied Realism*
Traditional vs. Progressive Schools	Self-Directed Learning Communities
Nature vs. Nurture	Serve & Return Developmental Dialogue**
Random Tinkering (Accumulating Small Changes) vs. System-Destroying Revolution	Remodeling Systems**
High Stakes Accountability vs. Unmeasurable Qualities	Scientifically Validated Measures of Well-being in Schools (e.g. The Hope Survey***)
Authoritarian vs. Permissive	Need-Supportive

Sink or Swim vs. Trophies for Everyone	Inspired Resourcefulness
Controlling vs. Unstructured	Autonomy Supportive
Big Brother vs. Hippy Commune	Nurturing Family (Mutually Responsive Systems)
Accountability vs. Evasion of Duty	Community Responsibility
Silver Spoons vs. Gangstas Paradise	Good Neighbors
Obedience vs. Chaos	Restorative Justice
Students vs. Teachers vs. Parents	Well Orchestrated Community Systems**
Teacher Autonomy vs. Teacher-Proof	Teacher Professional Capital****
Individual Will and Intelligence	Human, Decisional, And Social Capital****

* See the book *Philosophy in the Flesh* by George Lakoff and Mark Johnson
** These alternative phrases have been tested for efficacy in political discourse by the FrameWorks Institute with funding from foundations concerned with education issues (they were tested for their cognitive linguistic effects on mainstream educational dialogue, not with reference to self-directed learning. See http://www.frameworksinstitute.org/issues-education.html)
*** See the book *Assessing What Really Matters In Schools: Creating Hope For The Future* by Ronald Newell and Mark Van Ryzin
**** See the book *Professional Capital: Transforming Teaching In Every School* by Andy Hargreaves and Michael Fullan

To date, state and federal policy attempts to improve the core educational effectiveness of K-12 schools take the explicit curriculum to be the critical leverage point for effective change. Accountability schemes that rely on testing and standards consist of making ever more explicit, and often increasingly detailed, demands about how to better deliver and account for informational content. The policy makers are logically operating on a belief that if they get the right combination of precisely specified units of content to be delivered and instructional bookkeeping data about the units of content in the students' heads, then they will be able to tweak the systems of reinforcement to get better educational outcomes. Large-scale corporate businesses are intimately familiar with accounting for their inventory and tracking every detail of its manufacture, packaging, transport, and delivery. Given the combination of the default concept and the dominance of business interests in our current governance system, it makes perfect sense that the thinking of policymakers is limited to the concept that education results from the delivery of informational content. Unfortunately, for those policymakers, their naïve beliefs about education are causing more harm than good.

Causing Harm

On what basis do I make the bold, and likely offensive, claim that education policy makers are causing harm? I make that claim primarily based on the peer-reviewed empirical research of my predecessors in the field of motivation in educational contexts and on my own small contribution[12] to that body of scientific literature. For over 30 years, patterns of motivation in traditional non-self-directed schools have been studied repeatedly.[13] Amazingly, despite a variety of theoretical and methodological approaches, all studies have observed the same effect: declines in engagement or intrinsic motivation across the entire span of compulsory schooling. These observed declines are critically important and form the basis for my bold claim because they also indicate declines in the well-being of children.

Beyond my narrow field within psychology, others have observed similar patterns. Boston College developmental psychologist Peter Gray has written about the research of Jean Twenge that reveals the declining mental health of American school children going back to the 1940's[14] when appropriate measures were first used. The compromises to psychological well-being in schools are actually a global phenomena, according to a 2003 report entitled "U.S. Teens in Our World: Understanding the Health of U.S. Youth in Comparison to Youth in Other Countries".[15] The repeated empirical observations of a variety of scientists and surveyors have revealed that non-self-directed schooling consistently diminishes the well-being of children.

My research and the research of other groups that have been published between 2009 and 2013 show that self-directed forms of K-12 schooling actually maintain the well-being of their students.[16] The bleak picture from mainstream schooling raises the question for us self-directed learning advocates and practitioners, "How do we do that?" And equally important, "How can we adapt ourselves to have a much greater impact on the rest of the school system such that we can not only survive but thrive and grow?"

The Secret Of Our Success: Nurturing

"How do we do that?" "That" in this question refers to maintaining well-being, i.e. nurturing. Based on the theoretical framework (Self-Determination Theory) that I used for my research and how it applies to all human activities, I take nurturing to mean supporting learners to satisfy their primary human needs. "Primary" means that the needs are non-neutrally tied to well-being, are not derived from any other needs, and they are universal across cultures. You are undoubtedly familiar with the primary human needs for air, water, food, shelter, and sleep. To this list of physiological needs you need to add the psychological needs of relatedness, competence, and autonomy. Since the 1970's, there has been a robust and growing body of peer-reviewed empirical scientific research that supports the inclusion of these needs in the "primary" category.[17]

The Proper Role of Primary Human Needs in Education
There are an overwhelming number of narratives about education. And many of them probably have valuable and important things to say about some part of the educational enterprise. Given the proliferation of education narratives, it is difficult to decide which should be given attention and which should be ignored. I do not have an easy answer to that dilemma. However, I do have a suggested starting point. Let's begin with the idea of primary human need support as measured by the psychological well-being of the children being served in schools. I am not suggesting that primary human need support could provide an all-encompassing educational theory. Rather, I am suggesting that primary human need support should be a baseline foundation upon which any and all educational theory should be built. Notice that physics is built upon the laws of thermodynamics and the fundamental forces; chemistry is built upon physics, the theory of the atomic nature of the material world, and the properties mapped on the periodic table of elements; and biology is built upon the baseline foundation of chemistry, cell theory, genetics, and the mechanisms of generational genetic change.[18] In each of those fields, any contribution you try to make must be consistent with these foundational concepts in order

for anyone in the field to take you seriously. They are the current paradigms and they are mutually supportive of each other. Unlike those other fields, psychology has not yet arrived at a consensus of what could be considered a paradigmatic foundation. But primary human needs should be a viable starting point for it. The primary needs are the determinants of human behavior in the same way that the properties mapped on the periodic table of elements are determining factors in chemistry. Primary human needs are scientifically validated statements of human nature. Thus, in evaluating narratives in the field of education, it would be a good starting point to reject those that are not consistent with the support of primary human needs. The same pruning of need-thwarting dead ends should also be applied to all other aspects of the organization, administration, and practices of schools (regardless of their funding models, organizational forms, or legal standing). This is also how I would define equity in education, as the provision of access to primary human need supportive schools. Inequities are created when the organization, administration, and/or practices of schools thwart or neglect primary human needs.

So, how do K-12 self-directed learning communities maintain engagement and intrinsic motivation? We nurture children, in the basic sense that we effectively support the humans in our schools to satisfy their primary human needs. We do it in varied ways and in varied contexts. What is critical is that we know from robust empirical evidence with a solid theoretical foundation that for effective and efficient learning the psychological well-being of students is a causal factor, and thus of paramount importance. But, this is not an easy idea for most people to grasp.

Don Berg

Imagine that you are a parent and you and your whole family are in Independence, Missouri, in May of 1848. You are about to set out on the Oregon Trail, a 2,200 mile journey. You are preparing to spend four months walking beside an ox-drawn wagon carrying all your worldly possessions. Every time you stop, you have to unhitch the oxen, tend to them, and provide for all the other animals you have along for food or companionship. It means constant wagon maintenance, foraging for firewood and clean water, cooking over open fires and setting up and breaking down camp every day. You are risking the lives of your entire family. Disease, hostile people, wild animals, bad timing, and ill preparedness are all potential killers. Your odds of dying are 1 in 10. Yet, hundreds of thousands of people chose to take that risk by traveling along the Oregon Trail in the 1800's.

Now imagine that, back in May of 1848 in Independence, I materialize in front of you and offer you the following proposition: I have access to a flying machine called an airplane. It can take your family all the way to Oregon in one day instead of four months. The airplane will also reduce your odds of dying to less than 1 in 1,000. But the problem is I don't know when in the next four months the airplane is going to be available to take you to Oregon.

The question is: Which risk do you take? Do you choose the familiar wagon mode of travel? Or, do you choose the mysterious airplane mode of travel which some guy claims is much safer but operates on an unpredictable schedule and is unfamiliar? Based on the current understanding of how people make such decisions from psychology, experimental philosophy, and behavioral economics, we can be confident that most people are going to take the familiar option without even considering the odds.

The relevance of this imaginary situation is that we are promoting self-directed learning, an educational opportunity for families that is likely to be just as strange to most people now as an airplane would have been to pioneers in 1848. I will describe the substantial risks of the familiar route in K-12 schooling in a little bit. What we know about the long-term outcomes is that they are roughly comparable to mainstream K-12 schools. All the basic outcomes, such as being able to read, write, and do arithmetic will occur, but at an unknown time. They will happen; we just can't predict when. Regardless of the mode of transportation, those who survive the journey will end up in basically the same place. Some advocates and true believers might suggest I am understating the long-term superiority of their alternatives, but scholars are an intellectually conservative lot and they are not yet convinced of the long-term superiority of either mode. (See the comprehensive meta-study of home school research by Kunzman and Gaither and the various studies of the alumni of Sudbury Valley School.[19])

The new data from my study and the few others I found with similar results suggest that self-directed learning communities have a clear advantage along the journey itself regardless of long-term outcomes. The self-directed learning communities we advocate for support the kids' psychological well-being on their journey to adulthood, while mainstream schools systematically diminish kids' psychological well-being. But these alternatives are unfamiliar to most people. The evidence suggests that they provide the basics that everyone would agree are important, but the timing is unpredictable. New evidence suggests that they will reliably nurture children, but regular schools have the advantage of being familiar and we know that familiarity is important to most people.

This is why parents are on the horns of the following dilemma: Their parental responsibility in the world today is to find a school to nurture their children so they can live a normal adult life while their kids grow up to be awesome people. But school, the primary institution that is responsible for supplying and organizing child-nurturing people, has a system in place that actively interferes with the ability of the people in schools to do the nurturing job parents need them to do.

There are three major symptoms of this systematic lack of nurturing in schools. Two that everyone knows about are: dropping out and underachieving. The third major symptom that everyone understands but few acknowledge is "fauxcheiving," lacking mastery of the given subject despite attaining "achievements." These three symptoms reflect problems with systematic neglect of the primary human psychological needs:

- **Drop outs** are alienated from school instead of welcomed into it. So they disengage from the school. Their psychological need for **relatedness** has been thwarted. According to a report issued this year by the National Center for Education Statistics[20] in 2012, the drop out risk was the lowest for white kids (at 1 in 25) and was the highest for Hispanic kids (at about 1 in 8) with all other racial groups falling somewhere in between.

- **Underachievers** experience schools as a controlling place where they do not have adequate self-expression. So they disengage from the majority of classroom activities. Their psychological need for **autonomy** has been thwarted. According to the 2009 High School Transcript Study[21], also from the National Center for Education Statistics, 1 in 4 graduates are below curriculum standards.

- **Fauxchievers** experience schools as arbitrary systems to be gamed. So while they might seem engaged in school generally, they are mentally disengaged from some or all of their subjects and do an absolute minimum of work to get whatever level of scores or grades they deem necessary. Their psychological need for **competence** has been thwarted. According to Howard Gardner in his 2004 book *The Unschooled Mind*[22], at least 1 in 2 of those who go on to advanced degrees in their field do so by fauxchievement. This means that they are unable to solve the most basic problems in their field of specialization when those problems are presented in a real world manner, rather than how they would have been presented on a school test.

So, no matter how you slice it, there is a significant risk that the school system will cheat your child out of some or all of the education they deserve. They can be cheated in several ways, but the odds of being cheated are good if you stick to typical mainstream schools, regardless of whether the schools they attend are public, private, or charter. And marginalized populations run the highest risks (see Appendix 2: Why don't African-American children perform as well as white students in school?).

The acquisition of an education today in mainstream schools under the delivery paradigm is comparable to surviving disease up until the late 1800's under the miasma paradigm in medicine. There are lots of people who achieve the desired outcome, but the foundational idea that guides public investments in reform makes it more and more likely that the harms will be delivered more reliably than the benefits. The treatments of choice under the miasma paradigm were blood-letting, purging, and cupping. The idea was to rebalance the various "humors" that circulated in the body. The "curative powers" of these "treatments" were illusory, but for thousands of years, they persisted. The harms of the medical system were meted out consistently through the indiscriminate use of these "treatments," but any possible benefits of these derivatives of the miasma paradigm would have been the result of chance and luck. The successful healing of diseases was never properly attributable to those "treatments."

According to Eric Haas, Gustavo Fischman, and Joe Brewer in their book *Dumb Ideas Won't Create Smart Kids*[23], there is evidence that the concepts that have informed the design of schools has been fundamentally the same for at least 4,000 years, despite wide variations in how that concept was instantiated in the cultural institutions expected to deliver the goods. The intuitively obvious delivery metaphor has been deceiving everyone about the educative benefits of delivering instructional content in the same way that intuitively obvious ideas in medicine, like miasma and humors, deceived everyone about the beneficial effects of actions such as bleeding, cupping, purging, and removing bad smells. Both miasma and instructional delivery have had some incidental positive effects for some people, but the theories in themselves cannot predict who will be the beneficiaries. In education today, we force almost everyone into the industrial academic delivery machine in order to ensure some lucky few will attain an education. The public frets about the wasted human potential that results from the inequities. But our most powerful mainstream institutions have so far largely ignored the schools that may be modeling a truly equitable education. Our intuitions that the most important aspects of education are delivering and accounting for units of content delude us into taking societal actions that are not just educationally ineffective, but psychologically harmful.

The delivery paradigm has suppressed school practices that effectively put the primary human needs for relatedness and autonomy at the center of their educational communities. The Yale School Development Program has been getting substantive results by focusing primarily on relationships[24] and observed that their results could be undermined or destroyed by policies and politicking at the district or higher levels. Andy Hargreaves and Michael Fullan also describe how a school that had been identified as struggling made substantially positive reforms by supporting their primary population of at-risk children to have more artistic opportunities by transforming the entire school into an integrated arts program. Those reforms were later destroyed when policy decisions above the school-level[25] arbitrarily changed the measures of what counted as success. The destructive decisions made "sense" within the context of delivery theory because they insisted on imposing the same standards of performance across all schools, but the decisions were clearly counterproductive to a school community that had found creative ways to address the real needs of their student population.

The delivery paradigm has been effectively suppressing schools and other self-directed learning communities that support children to satisfy their need for autonomy for over 100 years. For example, in 1999 the British Office of Standards in Education attempted to shut down A.S. Neill's Summerhill School, which was founded in 1921. Besides having a long history, the school is also the single most famous self-directed learning community because A.S. Neill's book about the school sold over 4 million copies worldwide between the 1960's and the 1990's. The school was forced to raise hundreds of thousands of pounds in order to mount a successful defense of their right to maintain their pedagogical commitment to honoring the autonomy of the children in their care. Such an action makes it clear that operating a school with such a "radical" pedagogy may entail extreme financial risks if you expect to defend yourself against government attacks even with the benefits of global fame and over 70 years of supportive alumni. For the sake of the well-being of children and everyone else within the school system, it is time to cast aside the delivery paradigm.

Equity in education is a fundamentally important issue in a democratic society because a fully functional democracy depends on a substantially engaged citizenry. The causal factors in enabling human beings to be engaged are the supports for primary needs. James P. Comer, in the quote at the beginning of this book, observes that our society has failed to enable people to meet their basic or primary needs. The health of our democracy is at risk as long as this failure to provide equitable access to primary need supports continues. In regard to improving equity, there are several important points to keep in mind.

It is inevitable that some people will become educated when they are embedded in a society that provides access to learning resources. The interplay between a) the defective delivery paradigm that guides human behavior within the social system of schools, b) the hidden brain processes of humans, and c) the hidden dynamics of social systems ensure that the successes that occur within the school system are distributed with a certain amount of bias favoring the dominant groups while handicapping marginalized groups (see Appendix 2: Why don't African-American children perform as well as white students in school?). In schools designed for instructional delivery, there are only two systematic features that contribute to true education: 1) the fact that schools bring together a lot of people (thus inadvertently giving an opportunity for relatedness to be supported, but only if the right circumstances happen to occur), and 2) the statistical law of large numbers which ensures that the many variations in school design and management, plus the diversity of communities in which they are embedded, will inevitably produce some inadvertently good schools. Except to the degree that they inadvertently support primary human needs, traditional schools cannot deliver an education any more reliably than leaving kids in the care of their families as demonstrated by the homeschooling data.[26]

A variety of critics going back to at least John Dewey have long argued that mainstream schools inflict harm. The harms done are generally accepted as the given order of things, a natural and inevitable situation. In this sense the school system has always been bad. There has never been a "golden age" in which schooling was better than it is now in regards to predictably and reliably delivering an education to individuals. David Wootton, an eminent medical historian, in his book *Bad Medicine*[27], makes this same point of comparison for medicine in the pre-germ theory era. Given that delaying death and curing disease are the central defining goals of medicine, then the situation of medicine was always bad previous to developments of the antiseptic procedures, public health infrastructure, and public policies that accompanied the paradigm change to germ theory. Just because doctors could provide psychological comfort and administer socially accepted physical procedures then afterwards observe that some number of people got better, it does not follow that medicine was effective. Medicine as a system must be judged by its ability to reliably cure disease and delay death, not on its ability to maintain its status as a valued social institution. By that measure medicine did more harm than good before adopting the germ theory paradigm and it did not attain the status of being effective until after the germ theory paradigm became dominant. Until education achieves a similar paradigm shift, schools will continue to do systematic psychological harm to the majority of the children in their care, despite the fact that some few will become educated nonetheless.

But now we *can* do better than play the odds as a society. If we learn from the self-directed learning communities that have pioneered reliable methods of nurturing children and the scientifically validated model of the causal factors that contribute to human engagement we can accurately predict what investments will pay off in education. Successful schools need to be judged on their ability to provide support for primary needs before they should be judged on other criteria. There is no excuse for harming children in order to get content into their heads, get them into college, or get them ready for the job market. Anyone who makes that argument is complicit in harming children. They should have the errors in their thinking and the morally repugnant consequences of their argument pointed out. The conversation about equity in education needs to become about reliable access to primary need supportive schools as a higher priority than any other aspect of equity in education. The second highest priority in K-12 education should be meeting the developmental needs of the children, which the Yale School Development Program has been proving to be an effective element of reform for decades. All other considerations of equity should follow after primary and developmental need satisfaction have been supported. One of the consequences of adopting the germ theory paradigm in medicine was that previously unimaginable treatments that would have been miraculous under the previous paradigm became everyday occurrences; a comparable effect might occur if we can systematically deliver on the promise of equity in education.

When teachers acknowledge that self-directed learners allow them to be the most effective and efficient teacher that they can be, then those teachers are implicitly endorsing the necessity for the school environment to systematically support students to satisfy their primary and developmental human needs. There is no sustainable way for teachers to take on those responsibilities individually. Effective teaching is not a solo performance; it requires an ensemble, a whole orchestra, in fact. Everyone – teachers, school administrators, specialists, school psychologists, district administrators, consultants, secretaries, parents, policy makers, etc. – has to play their parts, or the result is a cacophony, not harmony. Teachers already want to do the right thing, but when the responsibility for nurturing falls on their shoulders alone, it cannot be sustained. Teachers should be **systematically** *supported* to do what they already want to do: nurture the children. That support needs to be orchestrated; the various players in the system need to play their parts in a coordinated way, not haphazardly and without coercion.

In non-self-directed learning communities, a.k.a. mainstream schools, the teachers are required to operate in an environment that systematically thwarts, or at least neglects, children's primary human needs. And it often thwarts their developmental needs, as well, as James P. Comer founder of the Yale School Development Program has observed.[28] And the system of justification for the design of those schools today is dominated by the delivery paradigm. That paradigm assumes that children have an educational "need" for information and does not take into account the idea that the humans in the system have primary and developmental needs that must be satisfied first in order for information delivery to be effective and efficient. That assumed "need" for information is driving the investment decisions of policy makers. As a result, those decisions are having unintended consequences, including the continuation of management practices that are systematically doing psychological harm to children.

Limits On Implementation

The framework of primary human needs provides not only the key to the solution to the systemic problem, but it also imposes restrictions on how the change can be brought about. It would be no good to thwart the needs of some of the humans in the system in an attempt to ensure the satisfaction of the needs of some others. It turns out that humans who do not have their needs met do a poor job of supporting the needs of others. Thus, it is necessary to apply a framework for primary human need support to the process of remodeling the system to ensure the implementation of policies and practices that reinforce primary human need supportive behaviors. The orchestra must be recruited to participate in the remodeling of the concert hall so we can all play our parts together based on a mutual commitment to the beauty of a harmonious system.

Catalyzing Systemic Change

Designing systemic solutions is the topic of my next book. But there are key issues that should be addressed in concluding this one. My concern is with the system of education for children in our society. I want all possible opportunities for educational experiences to be made available to every child in a manner that enables each of them, individually, to be reliably educated. Currently, our K-12 system provides parents with poor odds on that count. I want to address the deficiencies of the system strategically and recognize and honor the contributions of the vanguard of parents and schools that have already chosen certain tactics (which I've been calling "self-directed learning") to improve their chances of producing the desired outcome: educated children.

It is detrimental to our society if parents and schools act only on their narrow self-interests. Parents who believe in the value of public schools, but also observe the detrimental outcomes that the public school portion of the education system usually produces, recognize this dilemma. The actions of parents on behalf of their children could be helpful to the system if the system were organized to react productively to the choices made by parents. Currently there is no way for systemic transformation to result from the choices that parents make. Ideological references to "the hand of the free market" do nothing to drive meaningful large-scale changes of policy and practice. "Free market" magical thinking does a great disservice to our children. Another form of magical thinking is the unreflective commitment to public schools that does not tap into the potential contributions of private, charter, and home schools.

Neither free markets nor pubic schools can produce an educated child unless they are components of a public education system that transcends those narrow categories. Let's ditch the magical thinking and instead apply scientific discipline, where we identify causal factors that produce observable effects. Effective and efficient learning relies on well-being as a causal factor. As long as well-being is routinely compromised, then learning is also compromised. The preservation of well-being follows from the support of primary human needs, as decades of research into Self-Determination Theory and related psychological frameworks has shown.

Both public schools and free markets can contribute to a successful education system. In order to ensure that our education system serves our society, we need to establish a system that ensures:

1) equitable access to primary human need support across all races and classes with academic freedom regarding content (students/faculty level),

2) administrative freedom regarding the goals of particular schools and the processes they use to pursue their goals (school level),

3) a market discipline of holding each school publicly accountable to achieving both support of primary human needs and their explicit goals (district/EMO level), and

4) centralized protections for the well-being of all the humans in the system (with due process procedures at school, district/EMO, state, and federal levels).

At this point, we do not yet know what characteristics of schools are causal factors in the support of primary human needs. The observed declines in well-being have been documented in both public and private schools, which are presumed to share the characteristic of other-directed learning. The observed preservation of well-being has been observed in only a few kinds of schools which, so far, seem to share the characteristic of self-directed learning. Given that all of these observations encompass a vanishingly small sampling of the actual variety of kinds and characteristics of K-12 schools, it is not at all certain that self-direction is a causal factor. Much more scientific observation of schools across the spectrum from other- to self-directed learning needs to be done in order to settle that question.

But we do not have to wait for the science in order to do the right thing for children. Doing the right thing in this case requires a political movement. A political movement that envisions an entire education system that transcends the distinctions between institutional arrangements such as public schools, private schools, charter schools, and home schools. All schools contribute to the educative ecology of our society. All organizations that serve children are included in that system, too. Private businesses and non-profit organizations are included. It is time to think in terms of all those organizations working together to educate the children of our society by committing themselves to act on the scientific insight that primary human need support is the critical foundation for effective and efficient learning.

Before discussing the commitment directly, let me point out a couple of things about the current context in which that commitment is being called for. It would be an unmitigated disaster to simply try to change existing schools into copies of those communities that have already proven themselves to be nurturing. That would be like strapping wings on a wagon and expecting it to fly. If our existing K-12 self-directed learning communities are going to be replicated, the replications need to be well-supported start-ups, affiliates, or franchises of the proven models. (I would consider proven models to be ones that can provide evidence that they support the primary needs of their students.) Existing self-directed learning communities should start to consider how they could participate in replicating themselves. What kinds of capabilities or capacities do you need to be developing in order to fulfill that kind of role? What aspects of your work can be systematized, and what aspects need a more personal touch? What kinds of financial investment would be needed to make that happen?

Homeschooling Politics

Homeschooling parents have addressed their dilemma by directly acting on their fundamental responsibility to educate their children. Politically, homeschooling has been largely defensive, protecting the right to educate one's own children. It is time for homeschoolers to take responsibility for making the education system better, not just focusing on the education of their own children. It is not enough to lead by example; it is necessary to advocate for corrective action.

The choice of parents to educate their own children should continue to be protected as a right. Education by parents and their local community should effectively be the default in our education system. But, in the current situation in our society, it is important that all the other schooling options provide services that are at least as good as those that parents can provide their own children. The data suggest that mainstream schools are generally failing to provide a level of nurturing comparable to that provided by parents. But, as I pointed out at the beginning, nurturing children is not currently even in the conversation about education. That is how the self-directed learning communities can productively contribute to the conversation in education. Let's advocate together for making nurturing the first standard by which schools should be measured.

Remodeling K-12

Remodeling existing school organizations is the larger task ahead. The Yale School Development Program has been showing the way on comprehensive school reform for over 40 years and is relentlessly focused on relationships and child development. To improve on that excellent work I would suggest they measure patterns of engagement and/or intrinsic motivation to reveal patterns of psychological well-being. The Hope Survey[29] is one existing instrument that does just that. When engaging in a systems-remodeling process, we should take a principled approach instead of a prescriptive one, an approach I will describe in my next book. Dictating detailed instructions about how to change existing schools is a good way to thwart the primary psychological needs of those on the receiving end of the prescriptions. A properly principled approach, on the other hand, provides guidance without dictating specifics and requires the kind of involvement that is most likely to support the needs of those directly affected by change. And the most important litmus test of productive changes is patterns of improvement in the well-being of the children and teachers at the center of the system (and eventually all the humans in the system). Well-being should not be the only measured outcome, but it should be given the highest priority.

Lobbying

Enlarging the influence of our self-directed learning communities requires us to become visible in the public square and especially visible to public policy makers at school district, city, county, state, and federal levels. The best means to start gaining that visibility is lobbying.

The following approach to lobbying takes advantage of a combination of 1) a moral commitment to providing support for the well-being of the humans in schools, which also happens to be the true foundation of good education, and 2) the empirical evidence for the necessity of supporting both primary and developmental needs as the foundations of well-being. Given the political currency of the delivery model, it would also be important for lobbyists to educate the key decision makers about how education really works. The message to key decision makers, in simplified form, should be something like the following:

1. Well-being is the foundation of good learning; it is not a luxury, it is not an option, and schools cannot delegate their responsibility for it.
2. Between 2009 and 2013, three kinds of school were reported to have scientific data showing that they support the psychological well-being of the children in their care. Those are the only ones identified so far. We represent one or more (preferably all) of those models and their supporters. There are probably more schools that support psychological well-being, but we don't have data at this time to determine what other school models succeed at nurturing children.
3. Policies that are generated from the delivery paradigm of education diminish well-being. As evidenced by their consensus on the necessity of imposing testing and standardization, the policy thinking of both major political parties is dominated by the delivery paradigm. This is a trans-partisan issue because both sides are complicit in compounding the problems of our

school system. (We would be wise to develop and maintain trans-partisan support moving forward.)

4. The cartography theory of education combined with measures of the well-being of students can help us to develop policies that would reinforce the behaviors that are nurturing for children in schools.

5. You can be a leader in K-12 education by supporting our scientifically grounded innovations against those that are stuck in the rotten delivery paradigm.

6. With your support, we can orchestrate a remodeling of the school system that starts with replacing a rotten foundation. We, the advocates and practitioners of K-12 self-directed learning, can share what we do, help more people to understand why self-directed learning works, and enable anyone to apply the principles behind our work. Ultimately, together, we can create policies that systematically nurture all children, building on the scientific insight that well-being is the essential foundation for learning.

7. We would like to get your input on how best to proceed given the political realities you observe. We brought a resolution that might provide a useful starting point for our discussion.

The following resolution is written for policy making bodies that oversee the management of multiple schools. I encourage all K-12 schools and any other organizations that serve children to adapt this to their situation and formally enact the resolution so that the role of well-being in education can become common knowledge. As long as the resolution to collect school climate data that includes measures of primary need support is acted upon, then this will also start the process of properly studying all kinds of schools to figure out exactly what is necessary for doing right by our children.

Resolution to Build on Well-Being to Achieve K-12 Equity

Whereas, K-12 schools should be safe and healthy environments where all children are supported to meet their primary human needs (for air, water, food, sleep, shelter, relatedness, autonomy, and competence).

Whereas, neglecting or thwarting children's primary needs in order to deliver or account for academic content, give them job skills, and/or prepare them for college is harmful and should be avoided in educational settings.

Whereas, providing support for all students, teachers, and staff to meet their primary human needs (a.k.a. nurturing) is an equitable foundation upon which proper education builds.

Therefore, we RESOLVE to safeguard well-being by giving it precedence over the pursuit of other valuable educational goals, such as possessing basic knowledge and skills, job readiness, and college preparation.

Therefore, we RESOLVE to ensure that all our schools can provide support for all primary human needs because they are fundamental foundations for both well-being and education.

Therefore, we RESOLVE to ensure that every school provides an equitable foundation upon which each child's education can be built by requiring schools to assess school climate at least twice per year using an instrument that includes measures of psychological well-being and that has been validated through peer-reviewed scientific research, e.g. the Hope Survey.

Dissolving the Dilemma

The challenge is to make all schools meet a minimal standard of primary human need support. Why did the self-directed alternatives come into existence? Only because parents were forced into the dilemma. The move to making school climate a central defining metric of school success makes teachers responsible for a specific outcome that they have direct power to influence, unlike student performance on standardized tests of academic skills. School and classroom climate are factors that teachers and their managers influence substantially on a daily basis. With proper feedback about the climate of their classrooms and schools, they can make productive improvements by increasing their support for primary human needs.

I invite you to join me in advocating for primary human need support in every facet of our education system. This is the key to providing the missing nurturance in K-12 schools and will reverse the long standing trend that threatens to undermine our whole society.

Appendix 1:
Estimating Our Influence

How influential have K-12 self-directed learning communities been? I will examine the question of influence based on the relative proportion of the student population served in the United States of America. More influential segments serve larger proportions of the student population. This is a necessarily crude measure.

By my rough metric, public schools have been and remain the most influential segment in the U.S. since at least 1896. Department of Education statistics on historic enrollment trends since 1896 suggest that 1959 was a peak for national private school enrollment.[30] According to U.S. Census Bureau data going back to 1955, private schooling in the United States did reach a peak in 1959, serving slightly under 15% of children.[31] Private schooling has been in general decline in recent decades and was consistently under 9% from 2009 to 2012 (the most recent available data). In a 2010 report on all forms of "schools of choice" spanning private, charter, and homeschooling options, the percentage of the student populations varied from state to state with a range from a low of 3% in Alaska to a high of 17.6% in Louisiana.[32]

Charter schooling is the fastest growing segment of schooling in the USA, and it got started in the early

1990's. (Because charters come into existence at the state level, this glosses over a lot of variability, but their influence by my crude measure is remarkable either way.) Both charter schools and home schooling reached the 2 million student mark, or roughly 4% market share in the same year: 2011.[33] Public advocacy for the practice of homeschooling as a method for parents to avoid the problems of schooling started in the 1960's and research into it began in the 1970's. Private schooling is overall becoming less influential as reflected by its diminishing share while home schooling and charter schools are serving increasing shares of the student population. Charters clearly have been more influential than home schooling given their rise to a comparable level within a much shorter period of time. However, few charters can be considered to be self-directed learning communities, but to be generous to the charter school movement, let's put the number at 12% (approximately 240,000 students).

All other K-12 self-directed learning communities on the whole planet would not even give us another 1% of the U.S. student population in the most optimistic scenario (even if we include the generous charter estimate). To make the estimation another way, the total number of K-12 schools in the USA is on the order of 132,000[34], while the most optimistic estimate of the number of schools supporting self-directed learning would be on the order of hundreds, that is, three orders of magnitude fewer. The oldest self-identified democratic school in continuous operation dates back to over 100 years ago. Marietta Johnson's School of Organic Education in the USA was founded in 1907, and the most famous one, A.S. Neill's Summerhill in the UK, dates back to 1921.[35] Given that self-directed learning communities have been around in organizational form for over 100 years, combining the homeschoolers and all the other forms of self-directed learning communities for under 5% of market share and observing several orders of magnitude fewer schools indicates a lack of progress. But it is hopeful that the number of ways that children can access self-directed learning has actually grown.

In fact, it could be argued that support for self-directed learning should be at an all-time high. There are signs that it is gaining traction by other measures, such as a few foundations explicitly seeking to fund it (e.g. Nellie Mae and Hewlett Foundations), the substantial support of major foundations for Kahn Academy, the rise of Massive Open Online Courses, the major organizational recommitment in 2008 by Girls Scouts of the USA to actively make "girl-led" scouting a central defining feature of all of their programs, and the growth of "unconferences" like EdCamp for professional development.

Unconferences are gatherings of professionals in which the participants offer each other participatory workshops instead of the usual practice of relying on big name keynote speakers and sage-on-the-stage-style content delivery workshops. Unconferences came out of the technology sector at a time when their industry was so new that they realized there were no keynote-worthy superstars yet and the participants themselves brought the most valuable expertise into the room. Unconferences are largely self-organizing events. Event organizers provide guidance to participants by using a minimum of structure for time and space that encourages high levels of participation and personal responsibility for using the available time and space to effectively create valuable experiences. They are a form of adult self-directed learning community.

Consistent with the points made in the main body of this book, while these apparent moves toward self-directed learning are optimistic signs, counting on them to influence the school system would be misguided. The entrenched habits of thought that guide policy makers in their task of orchestrating the school system would undermine the potential influence of these examples. So, while it is encouraging that practices in diverse areas are converging on self-direction, there is great need for them to better communicate a shared understanding of what they are doing and why. Until they communicate more effectively, they will not have a lasting impact on the school system as a whole.

Appendix 2:
Why don't African-American children perform as well as white students in school?

(from Schools of Conscience E-Newsletter, December 2014)

People are always suggesting reasons why African-American children don't perform as well as white students in school. Some people say that it's their poverty. Some say that their parents don't value their education. Some say that the problem is that African American Vernacular English (AAVE) is different enough than the standard English most teachers use that there is a problem with kids' understanding. Others blame cultural resistance.

There are certainly examples of African-American students performing well in school, but all too often, their performance can be traced to the fact that their parents were interested enough in their education to send them to special schools, they are above average in intelligence, or their families are better off than their neighbors.

I would love to hear your opinion as to why this group--or any historically disadvantaged group you are familiar with--doesn't do well.

Peace,
Greg Burrill

Answer with a closer look at "performance":

Let's consider a parallel example. In anticipation of resistance to this example because driving and schooling appear to be in different classes of activity, I ask for a patient reading of my explanation before you judge the appropriateness of my chosen analogy:

People are always suggesting reasons why drivers from regions with high mean temperatures don't perform as well on icy road conditions as drivers from more frigid regions. Some people say that it's their perceptual abilities. Some say that their driving instructors didn't teach them properly. Some say that the problem is that there are too many variables in traction for different combinations of road conditions and vehicle features and maintenance for certain people to be able to handle it. Others blame cultural resistance.

There are certainly examples of drivers from regions with high mean temperatures performing well on icy road conditions, but all too often, their performance can be traced to the fact that they were sent to special schools, they are above average in intelligence, or their families are better off than their neighbors.

I would love to hear your opinion as to why this group doesn't do well.

First, it is perfectly reasonable to explain a lack of driving success under icy conditions in terms of perceptual abilities, training opportunities, and the characteristics of the roads, vehicles, and drivers. All the suggested reasons for the failures are certainly worth investigating and I would guess that evidence for all of them could be found. Those details are all relevant to a proper analysis of why a lack of success might occur. However, there is a solution to the problem that makes many of those details irrelevant. They are rendered irrelevant because the solution alters the causal chain of events at a link that precedes the point when those factors became relevant.

The plain language description of the solution is to explain the strategies of steering into the direction of sliding and how to properly use a very light touch on the brakes and then give the drivers a safe wide open space covered in ice on which to practice those strategies, preferably with some appropriate obstacles like traffic cones to help them fail safely and repeatedly, until they get the hang of it. A more technical description of the solution is to update the drivers' causal models for steering and braking under the contingency of icy conditions and then facilitating appropriate behavioral application of the causal models in a situation with minimal risk of damage and/or injury.

In this way of thinking, the most salient reason for the differences in performance are due to frequency of exposure to the conditions in question. It is simply a problem of exposure and having enough time to develop appropriate responses to that exposure. The solution to the problem is simply to provide the needed exposure and facilitate the development of appropriate responses.

There are two levels of response that are required: the systemic and the behavioral. The system level is how we create a situation in which the driver can effectively improve, update, or replace their causal model for driving in icy conditions. The behavior level is how we provide instruction, exhibit leadership, and give feedback during and after practice.

Here's how this analogous situation can be restated as a metaphor for the situation in schools: K-12 schools have been trying to learn without any guidance through mere trial and error to drive on ice under challenging traffic conditions. They have been crashing the car on a regular basis, and while the disadvantaged groups receive the worst injuries, the advantaged groups have a blind spot that prevents them from realizing how badly they have been affected by this situation. All of the potential reasons for this situation that have been suggested can probably be supported with evidence. However, many of those reasons may become irrelevant if the understanding of education can be updated and educational practices can be altered in accordance with that understanding.

Here's a relatively technical summary of what I am saying:

Implicit causal models have determined what measures of performance are used in schools. The implicit causal models used at both the system and behavioral levels in mainstream K-12 schools are currently wrong. Therefore, performance has been systematically mis-measured. Consequently, K-12 policies are mostly misguided and, due to human nature, systematically exacerbate the inequities that are already reinforced in the larger society beyond schools.

To finally answer your question: The reason for most performance issues in K-12 schooling is systematic neglect or thwarting of primary human needs, especially the psychological needs for autonomy, competence, and relatedness. The main reason for the neglect and thwarting of primary human needs is that the implicit causal model of education that informs the policies and practices of mainstream schooling ignores primary human needs. That incorrect causal model has also led to the high stakes use of measures of performance that would only accurately reflect the true performance capabilities of students who have had their primary human needs supported. Due to the neglect and thwarting of primary human needs, those measures are rendered useless and the high stakes attached to their use arbitrarily punishes those whose needs are neglected and/ or thwarted the most (such as African-American children). Thus, disadvantaged populations of all kinds are being victimized. Corrective action must begin with a concerted effort to pervasively support primary human needs. After needs are adequately supported, then performance should be re-assessed to find out how much inequity remains. Until needs are adequately supported in a pervasive manner, the typical performance measures are irrelevant.

In this way of thinking, the most salient reason for the differences in performance are due to frequency of exposure to support for primary human needs. It is simply a problem of exposure and having enough time to develop appropriate responses to that exposure. The solution to the problem is simply to provide the needed exposure to primary human need support and facilitate the development of appropriate responses. In the case of primary human need support, the development of appropriate responses involves becoming skilled at finding or creating and then maintaining connections to the myriad of societal systems that are available for supporting primary human needs.

A Closer Look at "Performance"

There are a variety of ways that performance is viewed in schools. There is a whole suite of traditional performance measures such as grades, test scores, rates of graduation, and so on. In the entrepreneurial circles that I enjoy, there is a new idea from Eric Reis that one of the keys to understanding the high rate of failure of new enterprises is the inability of aspiring entrepreneurs to make an appropriate distinction between vanity metrics and actionable metrics. Vanity metrics consist of data that gives the businessperson the illusion of knowing something useful. Actionable metrics are the opposite, meaning that they are data that give the businessperson clear information that logically leads to actions that can improve key business functions.

The classic example of a vanity metric is the hit counter on a website. In the 90's, when websites were a new and largely unproven channel for doing business, many web pages sported a little counter that indicated how many hits it had received. It is quite intoxicating for the creator of a web page to imagine that millions of people have hit upon their site. Unfortunately, this is not useful information. Most of the hits are actually robots that are just taking a quick automated glance and will never amount to any kind of productive outcome such as buying something. And even if you could filter out the 'bots, there is nothing inherent in the counting of hits to suggest what you could do to get the real human visitors to do something productive.

Actionable metrics, on the other hand, would be dependent on the business purposes of the website. For the sake of simplicity, let's assume that your site is selling some interesting product. What you need to know is not just how many people show up on your home page, but what they do after they arrive. If you find out they tend to spend only a minute on the home page and then click to an article you wrote about how your cat did something cute instead of the article about your product's benefits, then you have useful information and should reconsider whether the article about your cat is appropriate. Of course, if you sell some interesting cat products, then it might be just fine. The point is that you have to measure the potentially productive behaviors. It is not enough to measure any random behavior; you have to measure behaviors that matter.

Currently, the suite of traditional measures of performance in schools are vanity metrics. Humans have a set of primary needs that are causal factors in producing an education; only rarely have the supports for those needs been measured. There is no systematic awareness, let alone measurement, of how well human needs are being supported in schools. Measuring how well students' (and teachers') needs are supported provides actionable data because there are clear behavioral guidelines that specify what to do, and, just as importantly, what not to do, in attempting to support those needs.

The causal role of primary human needs in education is what is currently missing from both policy (systems level) and practice (behavioral level) in K-12. This book proposes a policy resolution that schools, districts, education management organizations, and departments of education can use to correct their understanding and reset their priorities in order to ensure that the correction gets appropriate attention and evokes appropriate changes. My next book will address 1) the design criteria for creating a situation in which need support is pervasive, and 2) the behavioral changes that are necessary for facilitating appropriate practice.

Endnotes

[1] Berg, D.A., & Corpus, J.H. (2013). Enthusiastic students: A study of motivation in two alternatives to mandatory instruction, *Other Education* 2(2), 42-66. URL: http://www.othereducation.stir.ac.uk/index.php/OE/article/view/31/60

[2] References regarding declines in engagement and intrinsic motivation-
Bouffard, T., Marcoux, M., Vezeau, C., & Bordeleau, L. (2003). Changes in self- perceptions of competence and intrinsic motivation among elementary school children. *British Journal of Educational Psychology*, 73, 171-186.
Corpus, J. H., McClintic-Gilbert, M. S., & Hayenga, A. O. (2009). Within-year changes in children's intrinsic and extrinsic motivational orientations: Contextual predictors and academic outcomes. *Contemporary Educational Psychology*, 34, 154-166. DOI: 10.1016/j.cedpsych.2009.01.001
Gottfried, A. E., Fleming, J. S., & Gottfried, A. W. (2001). Continuity of academic intrinsic motivation from childhood through late adolescence: A longitudinal study. *Journal of Educational Psychology*, 93, 3-13. DOI: 10.1037/0022-0663.93.1.3
Harter, S. (1981). A new self-report scale of intrinsic versus extrinsic orientation in the classroom: Motivational and informational components. *Developmental Psychology*, 17, 300-312. DOI: 10.1037/0012-1649.17.3.300

Hunter, J. P., & Csikszentmihalyi, M. (2003). "The positive psychology of interested adolescents." *Journal of Youth and Adolescence*, 32, 27-35. DOI: 10.1023/A:1021028306392

Lepper, M. R., Corpus, J. H., & Iyengar, S. S. (2005). Intrinsic and extrinsic motivation orientations in the classroom: Age differences and academic correlates. *Journal of Educational Psychology*, 97, 184-196. DOI: 10.1037/0022-0663.97.2.184

Otis, N., Grouzet, F. M. E., & Pelletier, L. G. (2005). Latent motivational change in an academic setting: A 3-year longitudinal study. *Journal of Educational Psychology*, 97, 170-183. DOI: 10.1037/0022-0663.97.2.170

Pintrich, P. R. (2003). "A motivational science perspective on the role of student motivation in learning and teaching contexts." *Journal of Educational Psychology*, 95, 667-686. DOI: 10.1037/0022-0663.95.4.667

Prawat, R. S., Grissom, S., & Parish, T. (1979). "Affective development in children, grades 3 through 12." *The Journal of Genetic Psychology*, 135, 37-49.

Vedder-Weiss, D., & Fortus, D. (2011). "Adolescents' declining motivation to learn science: Inevitable or not?" *Journal Of Research In Science Teaching*, 48(2), 199-216. DOI: 10.1002/tea.20398

Wigfield, A., Eccles, J. S., & Rodriguez, D. (1998). "The development of children's motivation in school contexts." *Review Research in Education*, 23, 73-118. Retrieved from http://www.jstor.org/stable/1167288

Reference regarding Jean Twenge's research on declines in student mental health:

Gray, P. (2013). *Free To Learn: Why Unleashing The Instinct To Play Will Make Our Children Happier, More Self-Reliant,*

And Better Students For Life. New York: Basic Books. pp. 1-20

3 Van Ryzin, M. J., Gravely, A. A., & Roseth, C. J. (2009). "Autonomy, belongingness, and engagement in school as contributors to adolescent psychological well-being." *Journal of Youth and Adolescence, 38*, 1-12. DOI: 10.1007/ s10964-007-9257-4

4 Comer, J. P. (2009). *What I Learned In School: Reflections On Race, Child Development, And School Reform*. San Francisco: Jossey-Bass.

5 National Alliance for Public Charter Schools, The. (2011, December 11). "Number of public charter school students in u.s. surpasses two million." Retrieved from http://www. publiccharters.org/PressReleasePublic/?id=643

6 Finnigan, K., Adelman, N., Anderson, L., Cotton, C., Donnelly, M. B., & Price, T. U.S. Department of Education, Office of the Deputy Secretary Policy and Program Studies Service. (2004). *Evaluation Of The Public Charter Schools Program: Final Report* (2004-08). Washington, D.C.: SRI International.

7 Johnson, S. (2006). *The Ghost Map: The Story Of London's Most Terrifying Epidemic--And How It Changed Science, Cities, And The Modern World*. New York: Riverhead Books.

8 Wootton, D. (2007). *Bad Medicine*. New York, NY: Oxford University Press.

[9]   Haas, E., Fischman, G., & Brewer, J. (2014). *Dumb Ideas Won't Create Smart Kids: Straight Talk About Bad School Reform, Good Teaching, And Better Learning.* New York and London: Teachers College Press.

[10] U.S. Department of Education, *The Education Department Budget History Table* Retrieved June 20, 2014, from http://www2.ed.gov/about/overview/budget/history/index.html

[11] Cartography theory is a synthesis based on my studies in psychology and experiences in alternative education. Key sources of inspiration for it come from Antonio Damasio, Daniel Kahneman, Daniel Siegel, George Lakoff, and Mark Johnson, amongst many others. It does not yet have a formal published expression, but rather is a work in progress. The following are some key works that have given me crucial insights:

Blakeslee, S., & Blakeslee, M. (2007). *The Body Has A Mind Of Its Own: New Discoveries About How The Mind-Body Connection Helps Us Master The World.* New York: Random House.

Damasio, A. (2010). *Self Comes To Mind: Constructing The Conscious Brain.* New York, NY: Pantheon Books.

Kahneman, D. (2011). *Thinking, Fast And Slow.* New York: Farrar, Straus and Giroux.

Lakoff, G., & Johnson, M. (1999). *Philosophy In The Flesh: The Embodied Mind And Its Challenge To Western Thought.* New York, NY: Basic Books.

Siegel, D. J. (2010). *Mindsight: The new science of personal transformation.* (pp. 52-55). New York, NY: Bantam Books.

12 Berg, D.A., & Corpus, J.H. (2013). Enthusiastic students: A study of motivation in two alternatives to mandatory instruction, *Other Education* 2(2), 42-66. URL: http://www.othereducation.stir.ac.uk/index.php/OE/article/view/31/60

13 References regarding declines in engagement and intrinsic motivation-

Bouffard, T., Marcoux, M., Vezeau, C., & Bordeleau, L. (2003). "Changes in self- perceptions of competence and intrinsic motivation among elementary school children." *British Journal of Educational Psychology*, 73, 171-186.

Corpus, J. H., McClintic-Gilbert, M. S., & Hayenga, A. O. (2009). "Within-year changes in children's intrinsic and extrinsic motivational orientations: Contextual predictors and academic outcomes." *Contemporary Educational Psychology*, 34, 154-166. DOI: 10.1016/j.cedpsych.2009.01.001

Gottfried, A. E., Fleming, J. S., & Gottfried, A. W. (2001). "Continuity of academic intrinsic motivation from childhood through late adolescence: A longitudinal study." *Journal of Educational Psychology*, 93, 3-13. DOI: 10.1037/0022-0663.93.1.3

Harter, S. (1981). "A new self-report scale of intrinsic versus extrinsic orientation in the classroom: Motivational and informational components." *Developmental Psychology*, 17, 300-312. DOI: 10.1037/0012-1649.17.3.300

Hunter, J. P., & Csikszentmihalyi, M. (2003). "The positive psychology of interested adolescents." *Journal of Youth and Adolescence*, 32, 27-35. DOI: 10.1023/A:1021028306392

Lepper, M. R., Corpus, J. H., & Iyengar, S. S. (2005). "Intrinsic and extrinsic motivation orientations in the classroom: Age differences and academic correlates."

Journal of Educational Psychology, 97, 184-196. DOI: 10.1037/0022-0663.97.2.184

Otis, N., Grouzet, F. M. E., & Pelletier, L. G. (2005). "Latent motivational change in an academic setting: A 3-year longitudinal study." *Journal of Educational Psychology*, 97, 170-183. DOI: 10.1037/0022-0663.97.2.170

Pintrich, P. R. (2003). "A motivational science perspective on the role of student motivation in learning and teaching contexts." *Journal of Educational Psychology*, 95, 667-686. DOI: 10.1037/0022-0663.95.4.667

Prawat, R. S., Grissom, S., & Parish, T. (1979). "Affective development in children, grades 3 through 12." *The Journal of Genetic Psychology*, 135, 37-49.

Vedder-Weiss, D., & Fortus, D. (2011). "Adolescents' declining motivation to learn science: Inevitable or not?" *Journal Of Research In Science Teaching*, 48(2), 199-216. DOI: 10.1002/tea.20398

Wigfield, A., Eccles, J. S., & Rodriguez, D. (1998). "The development of children's motivation in school contexts." *Review Research in Education*, 23, 73-118. Retrieved from http://www.jstor.org/stable/1167288

[14] Gray, P. (2013). *Free To Learn: Why Unleashing The Instinct To Play Will Make Our Children Happier, More Self-Reliant, And Better Students For Life*. New York: Basic Books.

[15] U.S. Department of Health and Human Services, Health Resources and Services Administration. *U.S. Teens in Our World* Rockville, Maryland: U.S. Department of Health and Human Services, 2003.

[16] References regarding maintenance of engagement and intrinsic motivation-

Berg, D.A., & Corpus, J.H. (2013). "Enthusiastic students: A study of motivation in two alternatives to mandatory instruction," *Other Education* 2(2), 42-66.

Newell, R. J., & Van Ryzin, M. J. (2009). *Assessing What Really Matters In Schools: Creating Hope For The Future.* Lanham, New York, Toronto, Plymouth, UK: Rowan & Littlefield Education.

Van Ryzin, M. J. (2011). "Protective factors at school: Reciprocal effects among adolescents' perceptions of the school environment, engagement in learning, and hope." *Journal of Youth and Adolescence, 40*, 1568-1580. doi: 10.1007/s10964-011-9637-7

Van Ryzin, M. J., Gravely, A. A., & Roseth, C. J. (2009). "Autonomy, belongingness, and engagement in school as contributors to adolescent psychological well-being." *Journal of Youth and Adolescence, 38*, 1-12. DOI: 10.1007/s10964-007-9257-4

Vedder-Weiss, D., & Fortus, D. (2011). "Adolescents' declining motivation to learn science: Inevitable or not?" *Journal Of Research In Science Teaching*, 48(2), 199-216. DOI: 10.1002/tea.20398

[17] According to Self-Determination Theory (SDT), autonomy, competence, and relatedness are primary human psychological needs analogous to how material nutrients are primary human biological needs. These needs, moreover, are directly tied to human functioning such that thwarting a need leads to ill-being while meeting a need leads to well-being (Deci & Moller, 2007; Reis, Sheldon, Gable, Roscoe & Ryan, 2000; Sheldon et al., 1996; Véronneau, Koestner, & Abela, 2005). Needs are called primary when they cannot be derived from any other needs, they are universally present in humans, and directly tied to human

well-being such that thwarting the need leads to ill-being while meeting the need leads to well-being.

Evidence for the claim that the constructs of autonomy, competence, and relatedness represent primary needs is based on two lines of inquiry into the causal relationship with well-being and universality (Deci & Moller, 2007). For example, two studies have supported the conception of the needs as psychological nutriments through daily diary studies that examined relations between measures of well-being and need satisfaction both within and between adult persons (Reis, Sheldon, Gable, Roscoe, & Ryan, 2000; Sheldon, Ryan, & Reis, 1996). In Sheldon et al. (1996) the measures of well-being included daily physical symptoms, vitality, positive affect and negative affect. The results from the well-being measures, both individually and in aggregate, were correlated with autonomy and competence as traits (where the person's consistent baseline levels of those perceptions were taken into account) as well as activities participants spent the most time on and their motivations for participating in those activities. The measures of well-being correlated significantly with most of the measures of need satisfaction as both traits and in the course of daily activities. The Reis et al. (2000) study focused on seven specific types of activities drawn from the literature as being associated with relatedness, using some of the same measures as used in Sheldon et al. (1996) plus a symptom checklist. Analysis provided strong support for the hypothesis that psychological need satisfaction is positively related to standard measures of well-being and negatively related to standard measures of ill-being. Véronneau, Koestner, and Abela (2005) established the connection between need satisfaction and both well-being and ill-being in samples of 3rd and 7th graders across six weeks using standard self-report questionnaires. They found that affect and the symptoms of depression were associated with need satisfaction. These studies provide direct evidence supporting the assertion that autonomy, competence, and relatedness represent human needs in that they are directly associated with well-being across most of the human age span.

The second line of evidence establishes universality through cross-cultural studies showing that the effects of these needs exist independent of culture. For example, in comparisons across the U.S.A. and Bulgaria (Deci, Ryan, Gagne, Leone, Usunov, & Kornazheva, 2001) and the U.S.A, South Korea, Turkey, and Russia (Chirkov, Ryan, Kim, & Kaplan, 2003), the researchers used common measures of need satisfaction: well-being as self-esteem, life satisfaction, work engagement, etc.; and ill-being as either anxiety or depression. In both studies, the authors were able to point out significant cultural variations in the conceptions and expressions of how the needs can be understood and satisfied, but the satisfaction still bore significant relations to well- and ill-being independent of those cultural variations on the theme.

References for endnote xvii:
Chirkov, V., Ryan, R. M., Kim, Y., & Kaplan, U. (2003). "Differentiating autonomy from individualism and independence: A self-determination theory perspective on internalization of cultural orientations and well-being." *Journal of Personality and Social Psychology*, 84, 97-110. DOI: 10.1037/0022-3514.84.1.97

Deci, E. L., & Moller, A. C. (2007). "The concept of competence: A starting place for understanding intrinsic motivation and self-determined extrinsic motivation." In A. Elliot & C. Dweck (Eds.), *Handbook of Competence and Motivation* (pp. 579-597). New York, NY: The Guilford Press.

Deci, E. L., Ryan, R. M., Gagne, M., Leona, D. R., Usunov, J., & Kornazheva, B. P. (2001). "Need satisfaction, motivation, and well-being in the work organizations of a former Eastern Bloc country: A cross-cultural study of self-determination." *Personality & Social Psychology Bulletin*, 27, 930-942. DOI: 10.1177/0146167201278002

Reis, H. T., Sheldon, K. M., Gable, S. L., Roscoe, J., & Ryan, R. (2000). "Daily well-being: The role of autonomy, competence, and relatedness." *Personality & Social Psychology Bulletin*, 22, 419-435. DOI: 10.1177/0146167200266002

Sheldon, K. M., Ryan, R., & Reis, H. T. (1996). "What makes for a good day? Competence and autonomy in the day and in the person." *Personality and Social Psychology Bulletin*, 22, 1270-1279. DOI: 10.1177/01461672962212007

Véronneau, M. H., Koestner, R. F., & Abela, J. R. Z. (2005). "Intrinsic need satisfaction and wellbeing in children: An application of the self-determination theory." *Journal of Social and Clinical Psychology*, 24, 280-292.

[18]   Also referred to as "evolution."

[19]   Kunzman, R., & Gaither, M. (2013) "Homeschooling: A Comprehensive Survey of the Research." *Other Education: The Journal of Educational Alternatives*, 2 (2013), 4-59.

Retrieved June 20, 2014, from http://www.othereducation. stir.ac.uk/index.php/OE/article/view/10/55

Gray, P., & Chanoff, D. (1986). "Democratic schooling: What happens to young people who have charge of their own education?" *American Journal of Education, 94(2)*, 182-213. Retrieved from http://www.jstor.org/stable/1084948

Greenberg, D., & Sadofsky, M. (1992). *Legacy Of Trust: Life After The Sudbury Valley School Experience.* Framingham, MA: The Sudbury Valley School Press.

Greenberg, D., Sadofsky, M., & Lempka, J. (2005). *The Pursuit Of Happiness: The Lives Of Sudbury Valley Alumni.* Framingham, MA: The Sudbury Valley School Press.

20   National Center for Education Statistics (2014, January 1). "Fast Facts: Drop Out Rates." Retrieved August 3, 2014, from http://nces.ed.gov/fastfacts/display.asp?id=16

21   Nord, C., Roey, S., Perkins, R., Lyons, M., Lemanski, N., Brown, J., and Schuknecht, J. (2011). *The Nation's Report Card: America's High School Graduates* (NCES 2011-462). U.S. Department of Education, National Center for Education Statistics. Washington, DC: U.S. Government Printing Office.

22   Gardner, H. (2004). *The Unschooled Mind: How Children Think And How Schools Should Teach* (Tenth anniversary ed.). New York: Basic Books.

23   Haas, E., Fischman, G., & Brewer, J. (2014). *Dumb Ideas Won't Create Smart Kids: Straight Talk About Bad School Reform, Good Teaching, And Better Learning.* New York and London: Teachers College Press.

24   Comer, J. P. (2009). *What I Learned In School: Reflections On Race, Child Development, And School Reform.* San Francisco: Jossey-Bass.
      Comer, J.P., Haynes, N.M., Joyner, E.T., & Ben-Avie, M. (1996). *Rallying the whole village the Comer process for reforming education.* New York: Teachers College Press.

25   Hargreaves, A., & Fullan, M. (2012). "Competing Views of Teaching." In *Professional capital: Transforming teaching in every school* (pp. 10-23). New York: Teachers College Press.

26   Kunzman, R., & Gaither, M. (2013). "Homeschooling: A Comprehensive Survey of the Research." *Other Education: The Journal of Educational Alternatives, 2 (2013)*, 4-59. Retrieved June 20, 2014, from http://www.othereducation. stir.ac.uk/index.php/OE/article/view/10/55

27   Wootton, D. (2007). *Bad Medicine.* New York, NY: Oxford University Press.

28   Comer, J. P. (2009). *What I Learned In School: Reflections On Race, Child Development, And School Reform.* San Francisco: Jossey-Bass.

29   Newell, R. J., & Van Ryzin, M. J. (2009). *Assessing What Really Matters In Schools: Creating Hope For The Future.* Lanham, New York, Toronto, Plymouth, UK: Rowan & Littlefield Education.

30   U.S. Department of Education, National Center for Education Statistics, *Annual Report of the Commissioner of Education*, 1870 to 1910; *Biennial Survey of Education in the United States*, 1919-20 through 1949-50; *Statistics of Public*

Elementary and Secondary School Systems, 1959 through 1980; Common Core of Data (CCD), "State Nonfiscal Survey of Public Elementary and Secondary Education," 1981-82 through 2010-11; Parent and Family Involvement in Education Survey of the National Household Education Surveys Program (PFI-NHES:2007); Private School Universe Survey (PSS), 1989-90 through 2009-10; *Projections of Education Statistics to 2021*; Opening (Fall) Enrollment in Higher Education, 1959; Higher Education General Information Survey (HEGIS), "Fall Enrollment in Institutions of Higher Education" surveys, 1969 through 1985; Integrated Postsecondary Education Data System (IPEDS), "Fall Enrollment Survey" (IPEDS-EF:86-99); and IPEDS Spring 2001 through Spring 2012, Enrollment component. (This table was prepared January 2013.) Retrieved June 20, 2014, from http://nces.ed.gov/programs/digest/d12/tables/dt12_003.asp

[31] U.S. Census Bureau – Housing and Household Economic Statistics Division, *School Enrollment of the Population 3 Years Old and Over, by Level and Control of School, Race, and Hispanic Origin: October 1955 to 2012* Retrieved June 20, 2014, from http://www.census.gov/hhes/school/data/cps/historical/TableA-1.xls

[32] Stoops, T. (2012) "Educational Market Share: Despite the growth of school choice, public schools dominate." John Locke Foundation Policy Report. Retrieved from http://www.johnlocke.org/acrobat/policyReports/EducationalMarketShare.pdf

[33] Home School Legal Defense Association, (2011, January 4). "Over two million children are homeschooled." Retrieved from http://www.hslda.org/docs/media/2011/201101140.asp National Alliance for Public Charter Schools, The. (2011, December 11). "Number of public charter school students in u.s. surpasses two million." Retrieved from http://www.publiccharters.org/PressReleasePublic/?id=643

[34] U.S. Department of Education, National Center for Education Statistics, Digest of Education Statistics, *Table 98. Number of public school districts and public and private elementary and secondary schools: Selected years, 1869-70 through 2010-11* Retrieved September 10, 2014, from http://nces.ed.gov/programs/digest/d12/tables/dt12_098.asp

[35] Berg, D.A. (2012). *Enthusiastic Students: The Motivational Consequences Of Non-Mandatory Instruction.* Reed College Thesis, p. 17. URL: http://www.teach-kids-attitude-1st.com/support-files/Don-Berg-Thesis-Enthusiastic-Students.pdf

About the Author

Don Berg is an education psychology researcher, alternative education practitioner and author, and has been active in local and state politics. The peer-reviewed journals *Other Education* and *The Journal Of The Experimental Analysis Of Behavior* have published his research. He has over 20 years of experience leading children in self-directed educational settings. He is also the founder of Schools of Conscience, an organization on a mission to build the nurturing capacity of all K-12 schools. For about a decade he has been involved in politics in volunteer and paid positions in Washington and Oregon. He currently lives at the Joyful Llama Ranch in West Linn, Oregon.